CREATE ENGAGING

LEARNING EXPERIENCES

FOR ADULTS

A Guide Book for
Speakers, Trainers, and Facilitators

About the Author

Mindy McCorkle has held a multitude of positions in her career: Director of Operations, General Manager, Vice President, and Executive VP. So, she knows a thing or two about leadership and business management! After racking up 30+ years of leadership experience in restaurant operations and property management, Mindy McCorkle embarked on career #3 by forming Enhancement Talent Development in late 2013. Enhancement is a training, coaching, and consulting company that focuses on helping others enhance their talent. Mindy teaches courses for trade associations, holds several property management designations, has coached and trained countless professionals, and does motivational keynote presentations for organizations across the country.

She has a long list of awards and has been facilitating learning experiences and coaching others for decades.

While running Enhancement Talent Development is more than a full-time job since she's a one-man show, she wanted to broaden her reach. In early 2017, Mindy launched Life. Enhanced. – a subsidiary of Enhancement. Life. Enhanced. focuses on helping others live more satisfying and successful lives by providing articles, resources, digital products, and freebies to help motivate and inspire others (and herself) to be their best self. This eBook is part of her journey to help others enhance their talent and achieve greater success.

Contact the author:
mindy@enhancementTD.com
www.enhancementTD.com
http://yourlifeenhanced.net

Preface

After doing several different presentations for different clients recently, I was feeling especially proud of myself. I have been on a quest for the last few years to provide *learning experiences* versus training. Last week, I had 3 different participants tell me that they enjoyed the 'experience' I provided for them.

They enjoyed the 'experience.'

That was music to my ears! They could have said they enjoyed the training, they could have said they learned something, they could have said just about anything nice, and I would have appreciated the kind words.

But to use that word – *experience* – well, it was just incredible.

I rode the cloud for a little bit, basking in what felt like a goal achieved. But I know I can never get complacent and that I have to continually strive to improve, no matter how good I think I'm doing.

So, I did what I always do at the end of the week: I spent some time reflecting on what I could have done differently, how I could do better next time, and what I did that I want to repeat. And that reflection process is what lead to this eBook. I hope you enjoy reading it as much as I enjoyed writing it!

Chapter 1:

What is a Learning Experience?

We've all been to training sessions where we were given a handout and listened to someone talk while showing a PowerPoint presentation. And we may have come away with some new knowledge. Sometimes though, we come away feeling as if we just lost a chunk of our lifetime. Yuck!

It's likely that we've all been to that dinner meeting or conference and listened to a speaker that was clearly there for the fame, not the favor. (I'll explain that in detail later!)

Hopefully, we've also been to training session where we came away feeling invigorated and re-energized. That's better than those other kinds of sessions, for sure. Unfortunately, chances are that initial psyched-up feeling didn't last long.

We can't always choose the training or conference session we attend – sometimes we're told where to go. (Ha! I just read that out loud and snort-giggled.)

Consider this:

The ideal LEARNING EXPERIENCE is one where you learn one or two pertinent actions that you can do right away in your real world that will have a positive impact on your success AND where you leave with sustainable inspiration that will move you to actually complete those actions.

Let's break that down.

A Learning Experience is an event or session where:

- **Attendees learn 1 or 2 PERTINENT ACTIONS**
- **Actions learned can be done RIGHT AWAY**
- **Actions learned are applicable to the attendees REAL WORLD**
- **Actions learned will have a POSITIVE IMPACT on the attendee's SUCCESS**
- **Attendees leave with sustainable inspiration that moves them to actually complete those actions**

Now, read that list again. It's a pretty powerful list, isn't it?

Why not rip out the following page and post it on your bulletin board?

A Learning Experience is an event or session where > Attendees learn 1 or 2 **PERTINENT ACTIONS** that can be done **RIGHT AWAY,** < are applicable to the learner's **REAL WORLD,** will have a **POSITIVE IMPACT** on the learner's **SUCCESS,** > and where the learner leaves with **SUSTAINABLE INSPIRATION** that moves them to actually complete those pertinent actions learned.

You see, when attendees feel that they have *experienced* the learning versus being spoon fed or worse yet had it shoved down their throat, they will remember the experience longer, and thus they are more likely to actually DO something with what they've learned. The pump-up that they leave with stays around a while.

As a professional trainer, volunteer instructor, or public speaker, you know how to do the first 4 things on that list. But the piece that determines the level of *experience* a training event offers is the last one. *Attendees leave with sustainable inspiration that moves them to actually complete the actions learned.*

THAT'S what this book is all about. THAT'S what creates LEARNING EXPERIENCES!

If you're in sales, you've probably heard talk about the importance of a positive customer *experience*. We've learned that when the customer has a positive experience during their selection process, they are more likely to purchase. Those positive customer experiences also create loyalty to your brand.

A few years ago, I started feeling the squeeze of competition. Other training companies had been in business far longer, so they already had a large customer base. While my business model is different from the typical training company, I needed as many advantages as I could get to continue to grow my small company. So, I started thinking about what I truly want to accomplish in the sessions I present.

Now, you may say the answer to that question should be obvious – they should learn something. And that's true.

But we all know that everyone learns differently, and when folks attend sessions because someone made them or just for a 'refresher,' the learning becomes even more challenging.

There are going to be participants who already know what I'm there to teach them, or who are not open to learning at all.

I knew I had to focus on the bigger picture: how I want those that attend my sessions to feel when they leave. And not just at that moment, but later, too.

The childcare arena has been talking about learning experiences for years now. So, I did some research and spent some time brainstorming about how to use the concept of an 'experience' in my sessions.

When I started thinking about all of this, all I could think of was one of my favorite quotes by Maya Angelou:

"I've learned that people will forget what you said, people will forget what you did, but people will never forget how you made them feel."

I felt like I was on to something.

So, I focused on making each session *an experience* versus a training event or speech.

Almost immediately, I noticed a change.

I started getting more follow-up notes from attendees and more referral clients. And I started feeling different after each session. I worried less about whether participants would retain what I had shared with them and more about how they felt about what I shared.

I've learned that people will forget what you said, people will forget what you did, but people will never forget how you made them feel.

Maya Angelou

The HOW starts in the next chapter, but first, let me share the benefits I've seen.

- The audience is more engaged early on and I don't have to work as hard keeping them engaged. Even those hard-to-reach skeptics participate without much prompting.

- Participants retain more of what they hear. I don't have hard stats to support this, but I do have dozens and dozens of notes and emails from attendees who have reached out to me days, weeks, and even *months later* to tell me how something they heard in one of my sessions improved their success, made their job easier, or helped them be more fulfilled.

- Attendees talk about *their experience* with others much more than they did before and that promotes residual learning!

- Attendees contribute to the sessions with their own experiences, thoughts, and ideas, and any time someone feels like they are PART of something, the experience meter rises.

Ready to get to the HOW? Let's go!

Chapter 3:

The HOW –
Preparing for a Learning Experience

Whether you're a trainer or speaker by trade or a volunteer instructor, the goal is the same – to share knowledge and to inspire your audience.

It's likely that you've attended some version of a Train the Trainer or public speaking training. And chances are, you learned about preparation. Creating outlines, scripts, and handouts. Gathering your tools. All that stuff.

And all that still applies.

But to create a true learning experience, it's more than that. It's about setting the stage for the experience.

We can do that by using the following 5 steps.

You are there for them, not the other way around!

Remember that fame-versus-favor comment earlier? This is what I was talking about. If you have accepted a training or speaking opportunity solely for what YOU will get out of it, you may not be able to create a positive learning experience. You may still give a great speech or solid instruction, but it won't feel like an *experience*.

For those of us whose livelihood depends on getting booked, it can be hard sometimes not to feel like you are there for a paycheck. That's especially true if you agree to doing a presentation that you don't really want to do because you need the money. I've been there, done that, and it makes it even harder to create an experience but it's NOT impossible. It just takes more work!

It drives me crazy when folks would act like there was some saint in our midst when a speaker or trainer would be present. I hear people introducing speakers by saying things like 'let's be respectful of our speaker and give her our undivided attention' or some other dribble.

No, people. NO!

It's not the audience's responsibility to listen to us. It's **OUR** responsibility to make them want to!

We are here **for them**. We must get over ourselves and remember that.

I recall being at a training session for a national company. The person introducing me asked the audience to put away their cell phones, so they could pay attention. Her name was Amy and she even made a comment to the audience about not checking their phone because that was rude to the speaker (me!)

Geez. Let me clarify. The people in the audience were *adults*. Professionals who had chosen to use their time to attend this learning opportunity. They CHOSE to be there.

Now, I understand that there may have been a few in the crowd that are present because their boss made them attend. But they were ADULTS too.

So, I adjusted my first few sentences to go something like this.

> I appreciate that introduction, Amy! And I'm glad to be here with you all. I know Amy asked that you put away your phones and pay attention, but I want to make you a promise. If I don't do my job, if I am not talking about something you care about, in a way that makes you want to listen, by all means, get out your phone and check your email or play a round or two of Candy Crush.

Why did I do that? Two reasons.

1) I wanted them to know it wasn't me that had asked for that message to be delivered. (OK, this one is a bit selfish.)

2) And so they would know that *I am there for them*, **not** the other way around.

Don't be there for the fame; be there for the favor of the attendees.

It's ALL about the AUDIENCE, my friends. You're just the lucky one who gets to spend a bit of time standing on stage or in the front of the room.

When presenting to adults, we should put ourselves in a *facilitator* frame of mind. We aren't teachers or even instructors. We are facilitators. We are *facilitating their learning experience.*

Often at a learning event, I'm asked, 'are you our instructor?' I answer by saying, 'no. I'm the facilitator.' I almost always get a smile from this answer. Perhaps it's because they think I'm being cheeky. But often I believe it's because *they get it.*

We need to be confident in our experience and knowledge, for sure, but if we get up there and act as if we are the utmost expert, or that we know everything, we'll lose half the group within the first few minutes.

It's likely that many of the attendees in your session will be very experienced in their field; some may even be smarter or more knowledgeable than you.

If we craft the learning experience successfully, they will learn as much from others in the group and from the experience as they will from us directly.

Now, in a keynote situation, it may be more difficult for them to learn from the others in the group as you may not have time for much interactive participation.

But they aren't likely sitting in the room for a keynote really thinking about how much they are going to learn. They are likely thinking more about how they are going to stay awake or how much they dread the rubber chicken most often served at those events.

We want their minds open to new ideas and new insight; and for that to happen, WE must have our mind open to the fact that we aren't *teaching*, we're **facilitating**.

Know your audience. **Really** know your audience. This will take some research on your part. But it will help you determine your choice of words, the organization of your content, and your areas of focus.

Now, for those of you in sales, you may be thinking, 'I do that all the time for potential customers when preparing for a presentation.'

Great! But this is a little different. You're aren't just looking for facts and figures. You're looking for culture, evidence of who they are as a collective group, and where their passions lie.

If you're speaking to or training for ONE company:

The research part will be easier. Go to their website and read their mission, vision, and values. Read their 'about us' section. Look on Glassdoor to see what employees are saying about the company. And then incorporate key words from those into your introduction.

Check out their social media presence. Use examples or anecdotes that correlate to what you see there.

Sure, you can ask questions of the person(s) you are working with to setup the event, but don't rely solely on that. Do your own research.

I made the mistake of preparing based on the organizers insight way too many times. Often, the person who is coordinating the event is in a different area of the organization than the audience members.

One such mistake happened when I was working with the COO of an organization who had asked me to do the keynote at the general session at their leadership conference. In my world, the COO would have a good feel for company culture, attendee engagement, and overall temperature of the organization. But that was not the case in this situation. Apparently, this COO was one who spends most of his time behind closed doors reviewing reports and analyzing stats.

He had told me that the audience – primarily shift managers and department heads – were highly engaged with the organization's growth plan and were fully on board with the restructuring going on.

As it turns out, the audience members knew very little about what was going on in the organization which was very clear from some of the conversations I overheard during the networking breakfast. And that was horrible because the premise of my whole presentation was that the audience was aware of the pain coming their way during the restructuring – but clearly, they weren't!

I should have asked more questions. I should have asked to chat with the other leaders in the organization, and maybe even a few of the department heads. At the very least, I should have thought about the possibility that the COO I was working with didn't really know what he was talking about. Now, I'm not saying don't trust what you're told. But you may want to take it with a grain of sugar – people like to present the internal picture with a layer of icing.

When you've done your research, incorporate what you've learned into your presentation. Don't say things like 'as your mission statement says' or 'since integrity is one of your company's core values.' That shows that you've done your research, but it doesn't add to the experience.

Instead, use the words subtly in your intro sentences to help the audience connect with you in a subliminal way.

For instance, let's say you're doing a presentation for Whole Foods about leadership. Their purpose statement says:

> *With great courage, integrity and love — we embrace our responsibility to co-create a world where each of us, our communities, and our planet can flourish. All the while, celebrating the sheer love and joy of food.*

So, in the first few minutes of your presentation, say something about courage, co-creation, and joy.

Some examples of how to do that:

You could use 'joy' in your intro. 'It's a pure joy to be here with such a dynamic group!'

When talking about the courage needed to be a great leader, you could say something like 'just like it takes courage to try something new, you will also need courage to lead' or something similar.

Perhaps when introducing an activity, you could incorporate something like, 'let's create a list of _____ together.'

You see what we're doing here?

I did a keynote at a client's annual leadership conference last year and used this technique. To be fair, it was an unusually fun group. I finished up right before lunch but I didn't get to eat because so many attendees wanted to talk to me! They treated me as one of their own, not just out of courtesy but genuinely like they knew me, and I knew them. That tells me this technique works.

If you're speaking to a group of mixed attendees such as an industry conference or symposium:

This research will be a little bit more difficult but do it anyway! Research the host organization. Understand what they stand for, who they serve, and what they offer to their members. Check out the companies and profiles of the key board members.

Use what you learn in your presentation. Again, subtly is the key here. Don't just mimic the mission statement or member services mantra – that's the cop-out way and they will notice.

And don't name-drop.

Let me say that again.

Do NOT name-drop.

It's fine to give credit to someone for an idea or quote. But don't throw out names of leaders in the group, or worse yet, attendees in the audience, just to make yourself sound connected.

Remember: favor, not fame!

If it's an annual event, dig into info about past conferences. Has it grown? Is it bigger or different than it has been in the past?

If you're facilitating a training session or certification program:

Ask for a list of attendees in advance. Identify male-female make-up if possible. Your presentation could be vastly different if presenting to a group of all one gender versus a mixed group. Your choice of stories or analogies may vary.

But remember, many names aren't gender specific so don't assume Chris is Christine because it might be Christopher!

If you are presenting to a group in your primary niche, you may be connected with some of them on Facebook or LinkedIn even if you don't really *know* them. Check them out if you can. See what their interests are.

Last year, I presented to a small group of commercial property managers and during my research, I noticed that many of them were heavily active in animal rights and rescue. So, I used that in my anecdotes and stories and they ate it up!

If there are attendees that you know on the list, reach out to them and ask them why they signed up for that particular session. Ask them about their primary goal, or what they are worried about. When doing this, resist the urge to make promises or assurances. Let them know you are just doing your research.

Ask the host what they may know about the attendees (level of experience, for example.)

And use all this information to develop not only your presentation but also the ice-breaker and activities you will use.

You may be saying, 'but wait, the topic is already set.' And that's OK. I'm not talking about the topic here. I'm talking about the *message*. In every great presentation, whether a keynote presentation or a training session, there are typically only 1 – 3 key nuggets - those statements that you want the attendee to remember if they don't remember anything else.

Let's take our Whole Foods leadership example again. And let's say we learned from our research that most of the attendees are proud of the healthy, natural life they live, and thus are proud to work for Whole Foods. They are likely *very authentic* people who value authenticity in others.

So, when talking about how a leader must not let his stress show, be sure that message isn't couched in a way that makes it sound as if you are telling them to 'act' like they aren't stressed. That could come across as disingenuous and that will be a huge mistake with the Whole Foods crowd.

Instead, ensure the message is more about how to camouflage or reduce the stress, NOT act like it isn't there. Make sense?

Practice. Not just once. Not just a few times. *Practice until you could do the presentation in your sleep.* Practice until you know exactly what slide is coming up next without even looking. Practice until it comes flowing out of your mouth with little effort.

I did a train-the-trainer presentation last fall and after it was over, the participants commented on how I never looked at the screen. One person said I must have magical powers!

Nope, not magic. PRACTICE! I practiced so much that I knew by heart which slide was coming next so with a few inconspicuous side-glances every now and then to make sure that my clicker was working, and the right slide was showing, I didn't have to look at the screen because I knew what was next and when to click the button.

Side Note: if using a handheld remote clicker (and I hope you do; any other way is antiquated and clunky!), practice with it ahead of time to ensure you know how it works. And don't point it at the screen when you click the button. That's not how it works!

Back to the subject of practicing:

Practice is critical, no matter how experienced you are.

I once heard a trainer say that practice was a waste of time; he said he could do better 'on the fly' without practice. I had seen his presentations and that wasn't true at all.

Without practice, rambling will likely occur and that can dilute the message. (That's not the only time you'll read that in this book. Rambling is to be avoided at all costs!)

Without practice, you'll be more reliant on your notes. If you don't use notes, and you haven't practiced, you *will* lose your place.

And you can almost bet that the lack of practice will shine through to the participants.

If possible, practice in front of someone. Recruit another trainer or speaker, family member or good friend to listen to your presentation. It won't matter that they may not know about your topic; you'll still be able to get feedback on flow, word choice, and presentation style.

This may sound daunting. And if you're like me and do a lot of presentations, it may seem like you have to spend a TON of time practicing. And THAT'S EXACTLY WHAT YOU SHOULD DO!

For every keynote speech I do (typically 40-50 minutes long), I spend approximately 3 hours practicing. For each ½ day session I teach, I spend at least 7-8 hours practicing. Now I'm pretty lucky, a lot of my presentations contain pieces from past presentations so I'm not starting from scratch each time. But even if it's a speech I've done multiple times, *I still practice because I always incorporate pieces that are pertinent to the audience.*

Don't worry about over practicing.

There is NO SUCH THING.

You may think that rehearsing too much will make you sound robotic. And delivering a canned speech will guarantee that you lose the attention of or confuse even the most devoted listeners.

But believe it or not, *practice prevents canned speeches.* When you are uber-confident in the material you're presenting, you'll be more able to add flare as needed throughout the session.

Create a Learning Experience

WITH THESE 5 STEPS

1.) REMEMBER THAT IT'S ALL ABOUT THE AUDIENCE

You are there for them, not the other way around!

2.) PUT YOURSELF IN THE RIGHT FRAME OF MIND.

We aren't teachers or even instructors. We are facilitators. We are facilitating their learning experience.

3.) KNOW YOUR AUDIENCE.

Really know your audience. This will take some research on your part. But it will help you determine your choice of words, the organization of your content, and your areas of focus.

4.) ENSURE YOUR MESSAGE ALIGNS WITH THE ATTENDEES' NEEDS

I'm not talking about the topic here. I'm talking about the message.

5.) PRACTICE

Practice. Not just once. Not just a few times. Practice until you could do the presentation in your sleep.

FULL DETAILS ABOUT THIS LIST AVAILABLE IN:
CREATE ENGAGING LEARNING EXPERIENCES FOR ADULTS: A GUIDEBOOK FOR SPEAKERS, TRAINERS, AND FACILITATORS

Available exclusively on Amazon.

For more details, go to yourlifeenhanced.net

Chapter 4:

The HOW –
Starting the Learning Experience Off Right

When attendees walk into the room for the event, they will decide within the first few seconds how they feel about being there. They may change their mind later if their first thoughts are of dread, but why risk it? Some of them may be there unwillingly so those participants are going to need even more to become engaged.

Start the learning experience off on a positive note by doing these 3 things.

Have all the setup completed *before the first arrival*. That means everything. All the handouts should be laid out in the chairs or on the tables. The slide deck should be queued up with your intro slide showing. Do all the audio testing prior to the first arrival. BE READY.

I know that sounds a bit trite, and it may be hard if you aren't given access to the room earlier enough but make a genuine effort.

Think about the times you've walked into a room for a presentation and heard the 'testing, 1, 2, 3, testing' over the speakers. Did that give you confidence that everything was ready? And that things would start on time?

I recently attended a statewide industry conference where one of the general session speakers was a nationally known name. Everyone was excited to hear him and were visibly excited while they waited on those mundane announcements that seem to be the standard at the start of a general session.

When the speaker finally walked up on stage, the crowd was pumped!

And then....

You could tell he was talking because you could see his lips moving but anyone more than a few rows away from the front couldn't hear a thing. He lavalier wasn't working.

Now, tech problems happen sometimes. But the speaker proceeded to tell us that he didn't know how to turn it on.

WHAT? If he had tested it, he would have known how to turn it on. There was a tech guy in the room, so he helped get the mic turned on quickly but not before the air deflated from practically the entire room.

That speaker was able to get the energy back up and recaptured much of the rooms attention. BUT later during the conference, I heard people talking about his session and people would say, 'oh yeah, the guy who didn't know how to turn his mic on.'

UGH. I don't know about you but that's not how I want to be remembered!

BE READY, FOLKS!

Finishing the setup while attendees are milling about will just add to your stress level and that won't help the experience at all – yours OR theirs!

And besides, you're going to need to be ready, so you can do the next step!

Interact with the attendees as they come in. That may sound like public speaking 101 and it is. But we want to ratchet it up a notch.

Don't just say hello and introduce yourself. That can be awkward for the attendee, especially if they don't recognize your name.

I remember doing that early on and one of the attendees say to me, 'what department do you work in?' He assumed that I worked for his company. Awkward!

Engage them in a *conversation*. Introduce yourself as a guest (because that's what you are!) and chitchat with them. Ask them where they came from that morning (part of town, or city, depending on the make-up of the group.) Ask them if they encountered traffic. Tell them you like their outfit (if you do.) Ask if they like that Android phone they are holding. ENGAGE THEM IN CONVERSATION.

As others come in, introduce the attendees to each other. Become part of the group. Create a sense of belonging among the attendees.

But watch for clues that some one may not really want to chat. Some folks may prefer to grab their coffee and settle into a seat without too much chatter. That's OK. Let them do that – after you introduce yourself!

If you're like me, many times, there are people in attendance that I know. Resist the urge to spend all your time chatting with those attendees. It can make others feel as if they are at a disadvantage because they don't know you. At the very least, pull others into the conversation so it's not just you and your buddy.

Remember, it's all about the audience!

Ask the host if you can introduce yourself. If that's not appropriate or the host wants to do it, provide them with an *abbreviated* bio to use.

Many professional speakers and trainers have an in-depth bio that their publicist or marketing firm wrote for them. That's great. Use it on your website or in your media packet.

But DON'T use it at a live event.

Leave out the long list of awards, or the names of all those large firms you've worked for or with. The attendees likely don't care about that.

What they care about is *why they should listen to you.* What *qualifies* you to be up front? It's the WIIFM concept. ***What's In It For ME****? How will I benefit as an attendee? WHY should I give you my attention?*

Fortunately, I get to speak frequently in front of people who already know me so introducing myself is fairly easy.

But when it's a group that is new to me, or may not be familiar with my background, I adjust the bio accordingly.

Let's say I'm speaking to that Whole Foods group we talked about earlier. The bio that I give to the host may look something like this:

> 'Mindy has 30+ years of experience in management, operations, and sales, and as you can imagine, she's learned a great deal about leadership in all that time. She's shared her experience with many companies and today, she's excited to be here to share it with us.'

It's short and to the point. It gives them a glimpse into my history and spells out why I've been chosen to speak to them. That's really all that's necessary at that point. I can help them get to know me a bit better during the presentation where it will be more conversational.

If I am doing my own intro for that session, it may look something like this:

'I'm Mindy and it's a pure joy to here with you today. Over the last 30 years across 3 careers, I've had the opportunity to make practically every leadership mistake possible. And I continue to learn every day. I'm honored to have this opportunity to share some of what I've learned with you!'

Again, short and to the point. It tells them I have ample experience, demonstrates that I don't know everything but have value to share with them and that I realize it's an honor to be chosen to be there.

You can add a personal tidbit but *only if it's pertinent*.

Here's what I mean by PERTINENT:

I am so very honored to have been given the Instructor of the Year Award TWICE by one of the associations where I teach certification courses. So, when I am in the presence of a group that knows of that organization, and I'm teaching a certification course, I may share that with the group to enhance their confidence in my ability.

BUT, when I'm with a group that I know doesn't know anything about the awarding organization or the certification courses I teach there, I leave it out. It just ends up sounding boastful when it's not relevant to the audience.

Other examples of pertinence:

A trainer I worked with in the past would sometimes introduce herself as a manager, mother, and trainer. Other times she'd introduce herself as a manager and a trainer. She'd leave out the mother piece when she knew that most of the audience weren't parents or were more reserved in their professionalism. She only included it when she knew that there were lots of parents in the group, as she knew it would help her connect with that audience.

I was speaking to a group of volunteers for a local animal shelter a while back and during that intro, I added to my bio that I was the proud mom to 3 fur-babies. I added it because it was relevant to the group and something that would help me connect with them.

An example of why pertinence matters:

I heard this story from a friend a few years ago and it stuck with me.

A speaker was hired to speak at a luncheon for a group of lobbyists. During his intro, the speaker mentioned that he was a master sharpshooter and had won several awards for his great aim. He went on to say that he liked spending his free time at the gun range.

What he didn't know was that there was a large group of lobbyists present that worked for CSGV. That stands for the <u>Coalition to Stop Gun Violence</u>. Yikes!

He clearly didn't do his research and let his ego get in his way. He was there for fame, not favor!

A good rule is to try to keep your intro, whether given by the host or done as a self-intro, to 3-4 sentences and only add 1 *pertinent* personal fact. Any longer, and people start zoning out. AND it's NOT about the speaker; it's about the audience! (Tired of hearing that yet?)

No matter how well you prepare, or how great you start off the session, it will all fall flat if the actual learning portion of the event doesn't provide a memorable experience.

How you convey your content throughout the event is what really sets a true learning experience apart from a training session or mundane speech.

Use the following 6 techniques to create an experience around your content.

Telling a story is a great way to engage – and entertain – the audience; and it can help demonstrate a vital point.

People respond to stories.

That's why many of us spend hours watching movies or reading novels – we love a good story, especially someone else's.

When you think about the enjoyable conversations you have, you'll realize that a lot of enjoyment and connection comes from when people share stories.

There are great storytellers and not-so-great storytellers. And if you are a not-so-great storyteller, you'll lose your audience's interest.

Stories must be:

- **Relevant to the topic.** You'll damage your credibility if your story doesn't tie into your message.

- **Short and simple.** Eliminate inconsequential details. If the story you want to tell requires too many intricate details, skip it and pick another one.

- **Timed well.** Don't tell too many stories too close together. A good rule of thumb is one story per major point. In a short presentation, stick with one story per 20–30 minutes of content.

- **Entertaining.** Don't add untrue details to make the story more entertaining. Authenticity is critical. Use tone, inflection, pauses, volume, body language, and facial expressions to make the story entertaining.

I have a blah story that I use in Fair Housing classes but by using some demonstrative body language, varying my tone and inflection, and inserting strategic pauses, I can see the participants hanging on my every word while I tell it.

- **Rehearsed and known.** It may be your story but that doesn't mean you shouldn't practice it. Know your stories by heart. If you flounder for the right words while telling a story, you'll damage the audience engagement and it could impact your integrity.

Note: It takes practice to be a good storyteller. We all know that person that takes forever to tell a story because they insert all those irritating details that don't matter. Or that keeps repeating the parts that she thinks are funny, even though you aren't laughing. PRACTICE telling your story. Practice it!

Ask a family member, friend, or a colleague to listen to your story. And LISTEN when they critique your storytelling ability.

If they tell you to leave out a detail – but it's your favorite part - leave it out! Remember, it's not about you or what you like, it's about your audience.

Be vulnerable in front of the group. This must be done in a non-arrogant, authentic way but sharing your own mistakes or failures helps the participants see you as a real person. It can help them feel less like the sinner sitting on the front row in church and make them be more open to really *hearing* your message.

Perhaps one of your stories tells about a major mishap in your life. Or scatter in a few 'I made that mistake' type comments throughout the conversation.

If you trip up during your presentation, own it. For example, if you mispronounce a word or use the wrong one, acknowledge it.

If you're a comedy fan, you may have heard Ron White's skit about flipping countries. White makes a couple of goofs in this bit where he mentions a *UFO* tour (as opposed to a USO tour) and a fence from the Gulf of Mexico to the *Specific* Ocean (not the Pacific). Instead of just correcting himself and moving on, he gives a funny facial expression and then continues to use those wrong words for a few minutes. Not only was that hilariously funny, it makes him *real.*

Don't go overboard with self-deprecation, though. That makes people uncomfortable and puts too much of the focus on you.

I worked with a super smart lady for a while earlier in my career and during the time where she served on the board of directors of a trade association, she frequently had to get up in front of the membership and make announcements or introduce sponsors or speakers.

While we loved her as a person, many of us would cringe when she would walk on stage because we knew what was coming. She was a big girl at the time, and she would always make some sort of joke about her weight, her big booty, something to do with her size. And while she would always get a few muted chuckles, many of those in the audience seemed to be very uncomfortable with her self-deprecating remarks.

Don't be her! Simply let the audience see you as less-than-perfect so that you'll be believable.

Speakers that talk AT the audience get fewer return requests than those who speak TO the attendees.

Trainers who speak AT the participants get lower evaluation marks.

Making eye contact with participants is one way to do this. We all know the importance of eye contact. And with small groups, it's fairly easy.

But with larger groups it can be difficult. We tend to think we need to make eye contact with each person, and that leads us to scan the room versus making meaningful eye contact with any one person. We don't want to leave anyone out, right?

We also don't want to spend too much time looking at any one person; that might make others feel like we don't want to look at them. And it can be uncomfortable for the one you're looking at.

But remember this: *these are adults.* They are smart enough to know that you can't look every person in the room directly in the eye for any valuable amount of time.

Don't do the scan thing. Make eye contact with those that you can for a second or two and then move on to someone else.

Using the power of the pause (more coming on that!), lock eyes with a few attendees while being silent for a few seconds. This makes the eye contact intentional and increases anticipation among the participants.

Another component of talking TO the participants is to engage them in the conversation. Ask questions and let participants answer. Ask for volunteers to share their story. Really create a *conversational environment*.

That's easier to do in smaller groups and when you have plenty of time. But it's important in every learning session.

If you don't have time for actual audience participation or the venue isn't conducive to that, try these tricks:

- Walk into the group and stand in various places. Use caution that you aren't shadowing over folks; that's uncomfortable and weird. Stand in the aisle for a few minutes. Or walk across the front of the room.

  More on movement in #6 later in this chapter! When attendees watch others following you around the room, they'll follow, too. It's that FOMO concept (the fear of missing out!) They want to look so they don't miss anything – and that increases engagement!

- If you're on stage, walk to the edge of the stage and lean towards the audience. This creates a connection with the audience and makes you seem like a part of them. (Be careful not to fall off!)

- Remember the part in Chapter 4 where we talked about chatting with attendees as they filter in? Use one of those conversations. Refer to the chat you had with Sarah or something that Jerry said to you this morning – IF it's relevant and adds value. And IF it shows Sarah or Jerry in a positive light!

Keep your focus on the audience. Gauge their reactions, adjust your tempo, volume, inflection, or movement as needed. And stay flexible.

Watch the crowd. Watching the group closely is important for a number of reasons but you'll be able to tell if they feel talked AT, versus talked TO by their body language, reciprocal eye contact, and the responses you get when you ask a question.

While you're in learning mode, watch a few speeches on YouTube and observe how famous speakers like Tony Robbins, Deepak Chopra, and Fred Thompson engage with the attendees. Watch how Talk Show hosts like Wendy Williams, Dr. Phil, and Ellen DeGeneres interact with their audiences.

It has taken me years to get comfortable with this, but it is so powerful.

Many speakers, especially those who are just getting started, or who get very nervous when on stage, tend to talk non-stop. You've probably heard someone like that. Unfortunately, like a lack of practice, that can lead to rambling and diminished clarity in your message.

Dead air, when unintentional, can be uncomfortable.

But when it's intentional – purposeful – it is very influential. If you listen to some of the great speakers out there, you'll see that they can hold their audience in the palm of their hand. The listeners seem to be sitting on the edge of their seat waiting to hear what they say next. And part of how those speakers do this is with strategic pauses.

David Hume, a presidential speechwriter and author, calls this the "strategic delay." He emphasizes that it adds weight and wisdom to the audience's perception of you. He believes that each second of pause strengthens the impact of your words. And I agree! I've seen it happen!

It takes more time to master the intentional pause so get ready for more – you guessed it – PRACTICE.

Start by sitting in complete silence and watch the second hand of a clock for 10 seconds. At first, it will feel like an eternity. But after you do it a few times, it will feel shorter and shorter. This exercise will help you understand that when it feels like you are being silent for an eternity during a presentation, it's really just a blip in time.

Then practice pausing. You can practice in the car. Practice with your family or colleagues. Practice when you are chatting on the phone. Practice, practice, practice.

Everyone is a superstar in some way. And most participants like to have their moment in the spotlight. So, let's give them that moment and reveal their superstardom!

Here's how you can do that:

Respond to correct or constructive answers with **positive affirmations** like 'exactly!' or 'wow! I like that!' or 'that's brilliant!' Try not to say 'you're right' – that will make it obvious when someone isn't right.

Respond to not-so-correct or irrelevant answers with **understanding**. 'I understand why you say that' or 'that's interesting; I hadn't thought of that!' or simply 'thanks for sharing.' NEVER correct an attendee outright in front of the group. It won't end well.

If you know someone in the audience that has something valuable to share, ask them to share it out loud. Don't put them on the spot though – ask ahead of time if possible.

Any opportunity you can give to attendees to shine in front of their peers will add to the experience.

Here's the DON'T that goes with this one:

Years ago, I was attending an annual awards event where the keynote speaker came out into the crowd and talked with individuals based on conversations she had with them prior to the event. It was going wonderfully – we were all mesmerized by her words and demeanor and couldn't wait to see who she would go talk to next.

And then it happened. She walked over to where our PIA was sitting (every company that has more than a few employees has a pain in the a$$, right?). The speaker walked right up to him and said, 'Based on our conversation earlier, I can tell you are a great leader and have a lot of influence in this organization.'

You could practically hear the collective gag spread across the room. No one liked this guy. He was arrogant and obnoxious, and I doubt a single one of us would admit to being influenced by him even if it were true!

So, don't do THAT!

Movement arouses the senses – both yours and the participants. Our eyes instinctively follow the movement. But you must move with purpose. No pacing. No twitching. Just smooth, purposeful movement.

When you move, the audience can't help but watch. When you stop moving, the absence of movement is captivating.

Move toward your audience and lower your voice to create intimacy.

Let your movements emphasize your message. When you're building up to a major point, walk briskly. When you reach the peak of a major point, stop abruptly.

If you are talking about something that's very serious or sad, squat down a little (but not so much that you get off balance or split your skirt!) This makes your presence seem smaller, so the audience will lean forward to keep from missing anything.

When talking about lighter subjects or funny stuff, use your arms and hands to demonstrate excitement and lightheartedness. But don't use your hands too much or you will distract from your message.

Move. With purpose.

Eddie Murphy once told Chris Rock to get moving! Murphy had seen Rock's stand-up performance where he just stood behind the microphone the whole time. And Murphy could see that the audience wasn't engaged. Chris Rock started moving from behind the mic stand and using his space and he has been rocking the stage ever since then!

In larger rooms, make at least one trip to the back of the room at some point. Otherwise, those attendees may think you don't even know they are there. AND they will be less likely to slip out early if they think you might walk back there again.

This can be hard in some situations, but I just make it part of my requirements when someone hires me. I have to be able to walk around the room. Period.

The experience doesn't end with your last words or when the applause stops (and there WILL be applause!)

It doesn't end until the last attendee has left.

That may be difficult sometimes; I understand that. But if at all possible, stick around until all the attendees have left the session.

Why am I saying this?

There are a few reasons I believe this is an important piece of the learning experience.

It shows that you are in it with them until the end.

Dare I say: favor, not fame?

It gives participants the opportunity to chat with you, ask questions, or simply say thank you. This is especially important if it's a longer session, a more complex topic, or a certification course.

It gives shy attendees the opportunity to come up and ask questions after most of the crowd has moved on. Again, especially critical for those more detailed topics or where an exam is involved.

It shows that you value the importance of your time there. Think about what it says to the attendees if you rush out right after your presentation.

You may think it makes you look high in demand, but it really just makes it look like you can't wait to move on to the next stop.

Remember, it's ALL about THEM. (Last time, I promise!)

I've seen times when the way the speaker left the room erased all the positive energy they had created during their presentation. And that's a shame.

Hanging around gives you time to bask in your glory (and catch your breath!)

If this is how you pay your bills, don't book so tight that you must rush out at the end. Adjust your prices accordingly if you have to but don't run out the door the minute you're done. How will you ever know what the attendees are saying about you if you do?

Last piece of advice for when it's over and you're chatting with those superstar attendees:

Don't act like you're glad it's over – even if you are!

I've seen speakers who were very nervous about the presentation show major signs of relief when their session was over. And I've observed how the attendees react to that.

I witnessed such a situation just a short time ago. A friend of mine was on a panel presentation and I went to give her moral support. She did a really good job, especially since I knew how nerve-racked she was. It was her first such presentation and I literally thought she was going to do a happy dance once her mic was turned off.

Several folks from the audience came up to her after the presentation and I overheard her say to them, multiple times, 'I was so nervous!' and 'I'm just glad it's over.'

I knew what she meant but I also saw the look on the faces of those in ear shot when she made those comments. While they said they couldn't tell she was nervous, I am pretty sure it impacted how they felt about her and the event as a whole. It impacts your credibility and status as a professional speaker when you focus on being nervous.

FINAL THOUGHT #1

Does it seem strange to you that the word 'student' doesn't appear anywhere in this book? In all 7,000+ words, not one time did I refer to the people you are presenting to as students. Did you even notice?

Why is that?

Because they are adults.

Not the first time you've read that on all these pages.

I believe that referring to adults as students creates the wrong mindset for us as presenters and for them. If we think of them as students, we'll likely think of ourselves as teachers or trainers. And we really should think of ourselves as facilitators.

Remember Step 2 in Chapter 3?

Sure, we call ourselves trainers, speakers, or instructors. Others may call us those things, too, and that's OK.

But just like putting ourselves in the right mindset (another Chapter 3 reference), we want the attendees to be in the right mindset.

And when we call them 'students' we may be impacting their mindset. We want them to know we see them as knowledgeable adults who have value to add to the event.

So regardless of what others call us, let's see ourselves as facilitators, and skip labeling those we spend time in our sessions as students.

FINAL THOUGHT #2

No matter how experienced we are or how much we practiced, occasionally we'll remember a pertinent tidbit we forgot to cover. And the temptation to insert it before we wrap up is often palpable.

But don't do it *unless* it *fits* in the conversation right that minute.

And by all means, don't say 'oh, I forgot to mention _____' as that not only dilutes your professionalism, it makes that point seem unimportant to the audience and many of them may go away thinking about how you forgot some of your presentation versus the main key point you want them to be thinking about as they leave.

In the back of the room after a general session at a conference I overheard a few attendees talking about the presentation. One guy said, 'gosh, that seemed like a pretty important piece of the puzzle; how could he have 'forgotten' to share that?'

I don't want to be that person.

And I'm betting you don't either.

FINAL THOUGHT #3

Set realistic expectations for yourself. If you go into a presentation expecting it to be perfect, you will be disappointed. I repeat – you *will be disappointed*. No one is perfect. And no presentation is perfect. So, don't strive for perfection because that is unattainable.

That doesn't mean you won't knock it out of the park! You will if you practice and adequately prepare and practice some more. But something – often just a little thing – will go wrong.

Focus instead on being the best facilitator you can possible be.

And let's get on with the process of facilitating engaging learning experiences!

I'll leave you with this quote: (because who doesn't love a good quote!?!?)

> *What we learn with pleasure we never forget!*
> *Alfred Mercier*

I am a firm believer in the concept of an Action Plan. I have all of the attendees at my workshops, training sessions, and seminars end the session by creating their own action plan.

I do this for several reasons.

1. When someone pays to be in one of my sessions (whether they pay for themselves or their company pays for them to be there), I want them to take-away tangible value.

   By creating an action plan based on what they learned, the value is greater, and they can't say later that they didn't learn anything.

2. When we write something down as an action item, we are effectively committing to ourselves that we will do it. Some sessions, it may only be 1 action item. In longer, more complex sessions, I may ask them to make a list of 3-4 items.

   Never more than 4 because, well, that would be unrealistic.

3. Having a written action plan at the end of the learning experience aids in residual learning. When we do something different that the way we've always done it, that in itself is learning. When we do it days or weeks after the session, the residual impact continues on. And THAT'S a facilitators dream come true!

So, here's what you have to do next!

Create YOUR Action Plan!

On the next several pages, choose the 2-3 items you want to work on first to enhance your facilitation skills and get you closer to creating true learning experiences for your attendees.

Specific Goal #1:

_____

_____

How will I measure success with this goal?

_____

_____

_____

_____

How will I achieve this goal? What steps will I take? What do I need to do differently?

_____

_____

_____

_____

_____

_____

How will this goal enhance my skills? What impact do I expect to see to my level of success?

_____

_____

_____

_____

What timeline is reasonable for this goal? When do I plan on completing this item?

_____

_____

_____

_____

_____

After starting work on this goal, how are things going? What has worked so far? What impact have I experienced? What needs to be done differently?

_____

_____

_____

_____

_____

What benefits have I experienced now that this goal has been completed?

_____

_____

Specific Goal #2:

_____

_____

How will I measure success with this goal?

_____

_____

_____

_____

How will I achieve this goal? What steps will I take? What do I need to do differently?

_____

_____

_____

_____

_____

_____

How will this goal enhance my skills? What impact do I expect to see to my level of success?

_____

_____

_____

_____

What timeline is reasonable for this goal? When do I plan on completing this item?

_____

_____

_____

_____

_____

_____

After starting work on this goal, how are things going? What has worked so far? What impact have I experienced? What needs to be done differently?

_____

_____

_____

_____

_____

What benefits have I experienced now that this goal has been completed?

_____

_____

Specific Goal #3:

_____

_____

How will I measure success with this goal?

_____

_____

_____

_____

How will I achieve this goal? What steps will I take? What do I need to do differently?

_____

_____

_____

_____

_____

How will this goal enhance my skills? What impact do I expect to see to my level of success?

_____

_____

_____

_____

What timeline is reasonable for this goal? When do I plan on completing this item?

_____

_____

_____

_____

_____

_____

After starting work on this goal, how are things going? What has worked so far? What impact have I experienced? What needs to be done differently?

_____

_____

_____

_____

_____

What benefits have I experienced now that this goal has been completed?

_____

_____

Made in the USA
Middletown, DE
09 May 2023

30282638R00035